1 MONTH OF
FREE
READING

at

www.ForgottenBooks.com

By purchasing this book you are eligible for one month membership to ForgottenBooks.com, giving you unlimited access to our entire collection of over 1,000,000 titles via our web site and mobile apps.

To claim your free month visit:

www.forgottenbooks.com/free953935

ISBN 978-0-260-52521-5
PIBN 10953935

This book is a reproduction of an important historical work. Forgotten Books uses state-of-the-art technology to digitally reconstruct the work, preserving the original format whilst repairing imperfections present in the aged copy. In rare cases, an imperfection in the original, such as a blemish or missing page, may be replicated in our edition. We do, however, repair the vast majority of imperfections successfully; any imperfections that remain are intentionally left to preserve the state of such historical works.

2F

CROPS AND MARKETS

FOR RELEASE MONDAY, APRIL 28, 1958

(Continued on following page)

UNITED STATES DEPARTMENT OF AGRICULTURE
FOREIGN AGRICULTURAL SERVICE
WASHINGTON 25, D. C.

CONTENTS (Continued)

ooOoo

U.S. TOBACCO EXPORTS
LOWER IN FEBRUARY

United States exports of unmanufactured tobacco in February 1958
totaled 23.1 million pounds, down 14.7 percent from February 1957. The
value of February 1958 exports, however, at $16.6 million, was only 7.3
percent below the February 1957 value.

Exports of flue-cured, dark-fired Kentucky-Tennessee, Virginia fire-
cured, and Maryland were well below those for February 1957. Gains were
noted for Burley, Green River, One Sucker, Black Fat, and cigar wrapper.
Burley exports, at 3.2 million pounds, were nearly double those for
February a year ago. Cigar wrapper exports were more than twice as large.

Exports of unmanufactured tobacco for the first 2 months of 1958
totaled 47.0 million pounds--a decline of 18.2 percent from the 57.5
million exported in January-February 1957. For the first 9-months of
the 1957-58 fiscal year, exports totaled 358 million pounds, down about
3 percent from the same period a year ago.

TOBACCO, UNMANUFACTURED: U.S. exports, by type and export weight,
January and February 1957 and 1958, with percent change

Type	February		Percent change	Jan.-Feb.		Percent change
	1957	1958		1957	1958	
	1,000 pounds	1,000 pounds	Percent	1,000 pounds	1,000 pounds	Percent
Flue-cured................	20,542	15,664	- 23.7	44,934	33,604	- 25.2
Burley....................	1,743	3,154	+ 81.0	4,112	5,389	+ 31.1
Dark-fired Ky.-Tenn.......	2,458	1,941	- 21.0	3,533	2,932	- 17.0
Va. fire-cured 1/	486	176	- 63.8	934	641	- 31.4
Maryland..................	632	498	- 21.2	1,324	1,469	+ 11.0
Green River..............	177	198	+ 11.9	382	209	- 45.3
One Sucker...............	95	212	+123.2	610	220	- 63.9
Black Fat, etc.	224	332	+ 48.2	315	678	+115.2
Cigar wrapper............	224	479	+113.8	418	724	+ 73.2
Cigar binder.............	91	78	- 14.3	157	547	+248.4
Cigar filler.............	29	7	- 75.9	29	8	- 72.4
Other....................	365	357	- 2.2	707	554	- 21.6
Total...............	27,066	23,096	- 14.7	57,455	46,975	- 18.2
Declared Value...........	17.9	16.6	- 7.3	38.9	34.5	- 11.3
(Million dollars) ......:						

1/ Includes sun-cured.
Compiled in the Foreign Agricultural Service from records of the Bureau of
the Census.

CIGARETTE CONSUMPTION INCREASES
SLIGHTLY IN SWEDEN

Consumption of cigarettes in Sweden increased slightly in 1957 to 5.9 billion pieces, up 3.3 percent from 1956. Cigarettes of domestic manufacture accounted for 89 percent of the sales, with the balance--about 0.6 billion--consisting of imported brands.

Cigarillo consumption also rose in 1957, but use of other products--cigars, smoking tobacco, chewing tobacco, and snuff--declined. Total usage of unmanufactured tobacco increased about 1.6 percent from 1956 to 1957; larger cigarette and cigarillo output was nearly balanced by declines in other products.

The increase in cigarette taxes that became effective April 1 is not expected to reduce sales. It may, however, prevent any significant gain in cigarette consumption in 1958.

AUSTRIA IMPORTS LESS
TOBACCO IN 1957

Austrian imports of unmanufactured tobacco declined from 30.9 million pounds in 1956 to 27.4 million in 1957. Imports from the United States dropped from 11.5 million pounds in 1956 to 5.2 million in 1957 and from 37 to 19 percent of total imports. Imports from Rumania, Hungary, Greece, India, Indonesia, and the Dominican Republic also declined. Imports from Yugoslavia, Bulgaria, Turkey, the Federation of Rhodesia and Nyasaland, Argentina, and Brazil were larger.

BELGIAN OUTPUT OF
TOBACCO PRODUCTS UP

Output of tobacco products in Belgium in 1957 totaled 53.0 million pounds--up 5 percent from the 1956 level of 50.5 million pounds. Output of cigarettes, at 10,546 million pieces in 1957, was 11.5 percent larger than the 9,460 million produced in 1956. Output of cigars and cigarillos also increased. On the other hand, smoking mixtures continued the downward trend noticeable for many years.

TOBACCO PRODUCTS: Belgian output, 1955-57

Product	1955	1956	1957
Cigarettes (million pieces)........:	9,165	9,460	10,546
Cigars (million pieces)...........:	111	127	135
Cigarillos (million pieces).......:	528	612	642
Smoking mixtures (1,000 pounds)...:	21,188	20,752	20,556

Source: FEDETAB

JAPAN USES MORE U.S. LEAF

Consumption of U. S. leaf tobacco in Japanese factories in 1957, was 9.1 million pounds, or 27 percent above the 1956 level, and nearly double that in 1955. This increase is attributed to larger sales of high-quality brands of cigarettes containing U. S. tobacco.

An intensive promotional project undertaken by the Japan Monopoly Corporation, the U. S. tobacco trade, and the Foreign Agricultural Service is believed to be responsible in large measure for steadily increasing use of U. S. tobacco. The percentage of U. S. leaf in several of the leading brands of cigarettes was increased last year. Various advertising media were extensively used to push sales of these brands--including "Fuji", "Peace", and "Hope". Sales of the higher-priced brands also have been encouraged by stepped-up economic activity.

CIGARETTES: Japan Monopoly sales of major brands to retail shops, 1955-57

Brand	1955	1956	1957
	Million pieces	Million pieces	Million pieces
Fuji 1/........................:	59	186	248
Peace 1/.......................:	5,863	7,092	9,989
Hope 1/........................:	---	---	2/ 233
Pearl 1/.......................:	1,737	2,680	2,171
Hikari 1/......................:	12,911	8,658	6,293
Ikoi..........................:	---	19,873	23,014
Midori........................:	---	---	3/ 1,334
Shinsei.......................:	49,046	42,283	45,931
Golden Bat....................:	25,968	16,660	10,691
Total.....................:	95,584	97,432	99,904

1/ Contain U. S. leaf. 2/ Placed on retail sale July 1, 1957.
3/ Placed on retail sale August 1, 1957.

Source: Japan Monopoly Corporation.

LIVESTOCK LOSSES IN BRAZIL

Large cattle losses due to drought have been reported in northeast Brazil. Conditions in the states of Ceara, Rio Grande do Norte, Parahiba, and Pernambuco are said to be unusually bad. Further livestock and crop losses are expected unless the drought breaks.

NEW ZEALAND CATTLE EXPORTS
TO U. S. POSTPONED

Trial shipments of New Zealand cattle, which were expected to begin
in May (Foreign Crops and Markets, April 18, 1958), have been postponed
for 60 days. The delay indicates that the economic and mechanical diffi-
culties involved in the transaction may have been greater than expected.
Whether any cattle imports will eventually be made from New Zealand is
not known. However, imports appear much less certain than previous information indicated.

WEST GERMAN LIVESTOCK
SLAUGHTER HEAVIER

Livestock slaughter in West Germany during 1957 rose sharply over
1956. Cattle slaughter, at 3,222,000 head, was 10 percent above the
previous year. Calf slaughter rose slightly for the first time in
several years. There was a sharp rise in cow and heifer slaughter, which
may indicate that West German farmers are reducing their herds.

Hog slaughter rose 4 percent over 1956. Owing to the large numbers of
hogs on farms, slaughter probably will continue large through 1958. Sheep
slaughter rose 9 percent, the first increase in several years. Horse and
goat slaughter continued to decline.

Heavy meat production has caused West Germany to reduce imports. The
percentage in slaughter from imported animals dropped sharply during 1957.
(For information on West German imports, see Foreign Crops and Markets,
April 21, page 9.)

LIVESTOCK SLAUGHTER: West Germany, 1953-1957

Year	Cattle	Calves	Hogs	Sheep	Goats	Horses
	1,000 head	1,000 head	1,000 head	1,000 head	1,000 head	1,000 head
1953.....................	2,669	2,702	14,473	796	86	127
1954.....................	2,852	2,640	14,664	689	91	122
1955.....................	2,888	2,435	17,295	593	86	94
1956.....................	2,932	2,274	17,737	546	83	91
1957.....................	3,222	2,308	18,796	597	76	73

Source: Statistische Berichte.

ANGOLA IMPORTS
U. S. CATTLE

Angola, Portugese West Africa, received a shipment of 22 head of Santa
Gertrudis cattle from the United States in March. Imported by a large commercial cattle-raising cooperative, these animals will be used to improve
native stock and start a purebred herd.

CANADIAN LIVESTOCK SLAUGHTER
CONTINUES TO RISE

Livestock slaughter in Canada during January-March 1958 increased over
the same period in 1957. · Inspected meat production rose 4 percent, from
471.6 million pounds during the first quarter of 1957 to 492.7 million
pounds during 1958. The largest rise was in hog slaughter, which increased
11 percent from the low level of January-March 1957. Cattle and calf
slaughter rose moderately, while the sheep kill dropped.

Due to large exports of feeder cattle to the United States during the
last half of 1957, fewer cattle were sold to Canadian feeders. Therefore,
the percent increase of cattle slaughter during the first quarter of 1958
was lower than in previous years. First-quarter 1958 sales of cattle to
Canadian feeders rose over those in 1957 and Canadian cattle slaughter is
expected to be much heavier in the coming months.

High hog prices and heavy grain production throughout 1957 encouraged
farmers to enlarge their breeding programs. Hog numbers are high now in
Canada. Slaughter is expected to remain high for the rest of the year.

CANADA: Inspected livestock slaughter, with percent change from
from previous year, January-March 1954-1958

Year	Cattle		Calves		Hogs		Sheep and Lambs	
	Number	Change	Number	Change	Number	Change	Number	Change
	1,000	Percent	1,000	Percent	1,000	Percent	1,000	Percent
1954.........:	396	+20	174	+34	1,152	-12	86	+11
1955.........:	399	+1	161	-7	1,400	+22	95	+13
1956.........:	431	+8	172	+7	1,532	+9	97	+2
1957.........:	451	+5	156	-9	1,336	-13	96	-1
1958.........:	461	+2	159	+2	1,420	+11	83	-14

Source: Canadian Department of Agriculture.

AUSTRALIAN WOOL SALES DOWN

Australian wool sales during July-February 1957-58 totaled 891.3 million
pounds--down 1 percent from the same period of the 1956-57 season. However,
the amount of wool remaining in store was down 23 percent from a year ago.
This reflects both heavy sales and a decline in production during the first
half of the season.

The value of wool sold during the period was $550.9 million, compared
with $669.2 million in the previous season. The average price declined from
74.8 cents per pound to 62.9 cents. Wool prices improved slightly the week
before the Easter recess, but were still near the season's low.

DOMINION WOOL PRICES
LOWER IN MARCH

Dominion wool prices dipped during March and were the lowest of the
season for all types. The monthly average price of merino 64's dropped to
the lowest level since September 1949, and crossbred 50's were the weakest
since June 1952.

Although prices had improved slightly for some types in January and
February, they declined from mid-February until mid-March. Some improvement
was noted in the last 2 weeks of March.

The South African Wool Board bought some 2,400 bales in March--its first
purchase this season. The New Zealand Wool Commission made it's largest
purchase of the season (940 bales) at Timaru on March 5.

WOOL: Clean cost, c.i.f. in the United Kingdom, based on
auction sales in the United Kingdom and the Dominions

Quality	March 1957	November 1957	December 1957	January 1958	February 1958	March 1958
	- - - - - - - - U. S. dollars per pound - - - - - - -					
70's	1.68	1.35	1.24	1.25	1.31	1.21
64's	1.55	1.25	1.12	1.14	1.19	1.10
60's	1.42	1.19	1.07	1.10	1.13	1.05
58's	1.28	1.13	1.03	1.04	1.07	.99
56's	1.23	1.02	.98	.93	.94	.89
50's	.99	.85	.82	.78	.77	.71
48's	.97	.83	.79	.76	.75	.69
46's	.95	.82	.78	.73	.72	.66

Source: New Zealand Wool Commission (London Agency).

VENEZUELA PLANS
SLAUGHTERHOUSE NETWORK

The Venezuelan Ministry of Agriculture has announced a plan for a network of slaughterhouses to be built throughout the cattle-raising areas of
the country.

The new establishments are to be financed by loans from a special
Ministry of Agriculture fund. The first slaughterhouse is expected to be
finished by next spring. Recommended by FAO, the program's purpose is to
ease critical supply and distribution problems of the Venezuelan livestock
industry.

AUSTRALIAN 1958-59 WOOL CLIP
MAY BE LOWER

The National Bank of Australia's latest monthly summary is not optimistic about the outlook for New South Wales' wool clip. Growth of wool
is said to be poor, and lighter fleece weights are expected from most
areas of the state. New South Wales is the largest wool-producing state
in Australia.

U. K. WOOL CONSUMPTION UP
SLIGHTLY IN FEBRUARY

According to the Wool Industry Bureau of Statistics, U. K. consumption of wool, production of tops, and deliveries of worsted yarns were 4
percent higher in February than in January, but down more than 11 percent
from February 1957.

The total amount of wool used in February 1958 was 37.5 million
pounds, compared with the January total of 41.1 million pounds. The daily
rate of consumption, however, was higher in February due to fewer working
days. In February 1957, wool consumption was 42.4 million pounds.

AUSTRALIAN CATTLE SLAUGHTER
MAY DROP

Poor rains in central Australia have made it difficult to move cattle
overland to markets this year. As seasonal movement of cattle southward
from the Northern Territory and Queensland has been delayed, total numbers
of cattle moved to slaughter may be reduced.

Australian cattle and calf slaughter rose sharply last year as producers liquidated herds because of drought. Exports of beef--especially
canned beef and low-grade cuts of frozen beef--rose sharply. If rains
continue subnormal, cattle slaughter and beef exports will probably drop.
(For data on Australian slaughter see Foreign Crops and Markets, March 31,
1958; on exports, March 10).

INDIA REDUCES CASTOR OIL
EXPORT DUTY

Effective April 8, 1958, the Government of India reduced the export duty
on castor oil from 175 rupees ($36.75) to 100 rupees ($21.00) per long ton.
The Indian oil trade had for some time been requesting a suitable reduction in
the 175-rupee export duty, in effect since April 1956, so that India might com-
pete better with Brazil, especially for the U. S. market (see Foreign Crops and
Markets, January 13, 1958).

On the same date the government reduced the duty on niger seed from 150
rupees ($31.50) to 50 rupees ($10.50) per ton.

NIGERIAN PEANUT PURCHASES SET NEW RECORD
OILSEED AND OIL EXPORTS LOW IN 1957

Commercial purchases of peanuts in Nigeria from the 1957-58 crop are now
estimated at 812,000 short tons, shelled basis. This is slightly more than
double the purchases from the 1956-57 crop. The 1957-58 transactions include
an estimated 22,000 tons of French West African peanuts that have been sold as
Nigerian. Over 95 percent of the 764,000 tons purchased as of March 14, 1958,
were "special grade" (70 percent or more of whole nuts).

PEANUTS (SHELLED): Nigeria, supply and distribution of commercial crop,
marketing years 1955-56, 1956-57, and 1957-58

	1955-56	1956-57 1/	1957-58 2/
	Short tons	Short tons	Short tons
Supply:			
Opening stocks, Oct. 1 ....:	---	---	---
Purchases........................:	593,900	400,960	812,000
Total supply.................:	593,900	400,960	812,000
Distribution:			
Exports..........................:	504,000	304,700	448,000
Crushings........................:	89,900	96,260	112,000
Ending stocks, Sept. 30.........:	---	---	252,000
Total distribution...........:	593,900	400,960	812,000

1/ Preliminary.   2/ Estimated.
Compiled from official and unofficial sources.

Exports of peanuts from the 1957-58 crop are estimated at 448,000 tons of
shelled nuts, about one-third above exports of the previous year. The record crop
has created a serious storage problem prior to shipment of the peanuts to ports
for export.

Lack of rail facilities to move the peanuts will leave around 150,000 tons of shelled peanuts stored in the open in pyramids of 900 tons each and another 100,000 tons stored inside when the 1958-59 season begins October 1.

Nigerian exports of oilseeds and oils in 1957 were, in most commodities, down sharply from 1956. Peanut exports were only two-thirds those of 1956, reflecting long dry spells during the growing season. However, exports of peanut oil were up slightly as a result of increased crushings by mills in the Kano area. Palm kernel exports were down about 10 percent, and edible palm oil exports in 1957 were about 15 percent below those of the previous year. Dry weather also probably accounts for much of the declines in these exports.

OILSEEDS, OILS, AND OILCAKE: Nigerian exports,
annual 1956 and 1957

Commodity	1956	1957 1/	Commodity	1956	1957 1/
	Short tons	Short tons		Short tons	Short tons
EDIBLE			PALM		
Peanuts (shelled)..:	501,854:	338,673:	Palm oil:		
Peanut oil ....:	39,320:	43,241:	Edible ....:	163,257:	142,095
Soybeans,..........:	11,424:	15,366:	Inedible ....:	42,206:	44,051
Sesame seed ....:	24,858:	19,206:	Palm kernels .....:	505,197:	454,924
Cottonseed ....:	41,818:2/	31,744:	Copra ....:	5,279:	4,068
INDUSTRIAL			OILCAKE		
Castor beans ......:	540:	643:	Peanut cake ......:	47,568:	47,047
			Palm kernel cake..:	857:	1,249

1/ Preliminary.   2/ January-September only.

Compiled from official and other sources.

HONDURAS CONSIDERS PLAN TO SUBSIDIZE
DAIRY CATTLE IMPORTS

A cattle breeders' proposal that imports of purebred dairy cattle be subsidized is now being considered by the Government of Honduras. This would indicate that milk producers and the government are interested in increasing the country's milk supply. Honduras is reported to be short of fluid milk at present. At Tegucigalpa, milk is selling for about 30 cents a quart.

NEW ZEALAND BUTTER PRICE
FALLS TO NEW LOW

The price of New Zealand butter, c.i.f. London, tumbled to 25.75 cents per pound, a 2-cent-per-pound drop and a new low level for recent years. The U. K. retail price for this butter will be about 30.2 cents per pound. The latest New Zealand price drop came after the Danish c.i.f. price was lowered 2.4 cents per pound to 27.5 cents.

MILK PRICES INCREASE
IN BUENOS AIRES

On April 1, new retail fluid milk prices in the Buenos Aires market went into effect. Converted to U. S. currency at the official exchange rate, pasteurized milk now sells in stores for 11.0 cents per quart. This milk is delivered to homes for 11.3 cents per quart. Unpasteurized milk, sold in bulk, is priced at 9.7 cents per quart. All of these prices represent an increase of 1.6 cents per quart from the prices in effect the previous period (September 1, 1957, to March 31, 1958) and will remain in effect until August 31.

Argentine producers supplying the Buenos Aires milk shed now receive the equivalent of $3.28 per cwt. Milk distributors are complaining that the present retail price increase has been passed on to the producers with no increased distributor margins. Producers, on the other hand, feel that any price increase is long overdue and only covers the increased cost of production.

U. S. BIRDS REVOLUTIONIZE POULTRY
MARKETING IN SWITZERLAND

The popularity of U. S. quick-frozen ready-to-cook poultry in Switzerland has been quickly recognized by the poultry industry. As a result, other exporting countries and the domestic producers are switching from "French-dressed" to fully eviscerated birds. U. S. poultry has also been generally praised for high quality, attractive packaging, and favorable price, but other suppliers are making every effort to become competitive in these areas.

Swiss complaints about U. S. poultry have been: (1) Too much variation in weight per bird. The Swiss would prefer a maximum range of 2 ounces, which would make possible a uniform price per bird. It is reported that competing suppliers are meeting this standard; (2) Too much water, resulting in discoloration and excessive weight loss; (3) Vent openings too large; and (4) occasional interior packaging.

COLOMBIA REPORTS LOWER
MILK PRODUCTION

Continuing drought conditions in 1957 in Colombia, which adversely affected pastures, caused milk production to drop below the 1956 level, despite a 3-percent increase in the number of milk cows. Output of butter declined 4 percent. Production of cheese, evaporated milk, and dried milk also was down.

CANADA'S EXPORTS OF
DAIRY PRODUCTS DECLINE

Exports of dairy products from Canada in 1957 were below the 1956 level. The principal factors in this reduction were a decline in the quantity of butter available for export and increased competition on the U.K. cheddar cheese market.

Approximately 60 percent of Canada's export trade in 1957 (and in 1956) was dried whole milk. In 1957, total exports amounted to 18.4 million pounds, compared with 19.3 million pounds in the earlier year. Cheddar cheese exports dropped sharply from 12.8 million pounds to 9.1 million pounds. Shipments of evaporated milk decreased 1.9 million pounds to 5.2 million pounds. Nonfat dry milk exports declined from 6.6 million pounds in 1956 to less than 1 million pounds in 1957. Exports of condensed milk, 2.9 million pounds in 1956, were less than 1 million pounds in 1957.

BRITISH GUIANA BANS IMPORTS
OF LIVE FLORIDA POULTRY

British Guiana has temporarily banned imports of live poultry from Florida because a recent shipment of baby chicks was found to be infected with Salmonella bareilly. This is the first case of this type of salmonellosis to be reported in British Guiana.

IRISH BUYING FIRST
U. S. APPLES SINCE 1956

The first shipment of U. S. apples to be received in Ireland since 1956 went on sale in Dublin on April 1. The Irish Government is permitting imports from the United States for a 3-month period which began April 1.

The initial delivery consisted of about 11,500 boxes of Extra Fancy Newtown, Winesap, and Rome Beauty. The Irish retail price is about 21 cents per pound, a lower price than consumers paid for top-quality domestic apples. Trade sources report that the fruit is of excellent quality and condition and is moving rapidly. Two more shipments, each of the same size, were scheduled to arrive on April 7 and 14.

WORLD BUTTER AND CHEESE PRICES: Wholesale prices at specified markets,
with comparisons
(U. S. cents per pound)

Country, market, and description	Butter				Cheese			
	1958	Quotations			1958	Quotations		
		Cur-rent	Month earlier	Year earlier		Cur-rent	Month earlier	Year earl
United Kingdom (London)								
New Zealand, finest-----	Mar.27	28.8	30.0	31.2	-------	-----	-------	----
Australian choicest-----	Mar.27	28.6	29.8	31.0	-------	-----	-------	----
New Zealand, finest white------------------					Mar.27	19.1	19.1	28.2
Australian choicest white------------------					Mar.27	18.5	18.2	24.0
Australia (Sydney)								
Choicest butter---------	Mar.27	46.7	46.7	46.7	-------	-----	-------	----
Choicest cheddar--------					Mar.27	28.2	28.2	28.2
Irish Republic (Dublin)								
Creamery butter---------	Mar.27	54.8	54.8	48.9	-------	-----	-------	----
Cheese------------------					Mar.27	30.8	30.8	30.8
Denmark (Copenhagen)-----	Mar.20	29.7	29.7	40.0	-------	-----	-------	----
France (Paris)								
Charentes creamery------	Mar.31	75.8	75.8	77.9	-------	-----	-------	----
Germany (Kempten)								
Markenbutter----,-------	Mar.26	67.0	68.1	69.1	-------	-----	-------	----
United States								
92-score creamery (N.Y.)	Mar.26	59.2	60.5	60.8	-------	-----	-------	----
Cheddar (Wisconsin)-----					Mar.26	35.0	35.0	35.
Netherlands (Leeuwarden)								
Creamery butter---------	----	---	49.9	49.9	-------	-----	-------	----
Full cream Gouda--------					Mar. 21	22.8	22.8	27.
Edam, 40 percent--------					Mar. 21	20.5	21.0	25.
Belgium (Hasselt)--------	Mar.27	73.0	74.7	82.3	-------	-----	-------	----
Canada (Montreal)								
1st grade creamery------	Mar.22	65.0	64.5	61.2	-------	-----	-------	----
Ontario white-----------					Mar.22	----	-----	35.

Source: Intelligence Bulletin, the Commonwealth Economic Committee; and the Dairy
Division, Agricultural Marketing Service, USDA.

FRANCE EXPORTS MORE
BUTTER AND CHEESE

France's exports of 22.3 million pounds of butter in 1957 were
more than double the quantity shipped in 1956. Principal markets
were Italy (5.7 million pounds), Algeria (4.3 million pounds), West
Germany (2.6 million pounds), Switzerland and the United Kingdom
(approximately 1.8 million pounds each). Other important outlets
were Morocco, French West Africa, Rumania, Tunisia, and Madagascar.

Cheese exports rose from 44.6 million pounds in 1956 to 57.5
million in 1957. By far the largest quantity--29.4 million pounds--
went to Algeria. Morocco took 5.5 million pounds, Belgium 4.0
million, French West Africa 2.7 million, Tunisia 2.6 million, the
United Kingdom 2.0 million and the United States 2.3 million. Exports
to the United States were almost entirely Roquefort and Blue cheese
(2.1 million pounds).

Condensed milk exports in 1957 were 35.4 million pounds, compared with 22.0 million pounds in 1956. Algeria was the largest
market, importing 17.3 million pounds. Other important outlets
were French West Africa (4.7 million pounds) and Madagascar (4.3
million pounds). Exports of evaporated milk at 14.0 million pounds
were more than double those of 1956. Algeria was also the principal
outlet for evaporated milk, taking more than half of total exports.
Dried milk shipments rose from 3.5 million pounds in 1956 to 9.0
million pounds in 1957. Approximately 2.5 million pounds each went
to West Germany and to Algeria.

French imports of butter declined sharply from 37.8 million
pounds in 1956 to only 1.4 million pounds in 1957, most of which came
from Denmark and the Netherlands. Imports of cheese also were down,
amounting to 23.6 million pounds, compared with 27.4 million pounds
in 1956. Important suppliers were Switzerland (10.0 million pounds),
Italy (5.5 million pounds), the Netherlands (4.6 million pounds) and
West Germany (2.0 million pounds).

CEYLON BYLAWS GOVERN
PUBLIC COCOA AUCTIONS

The Ceylon Chamber of Commerce on March 27 issued bylaws govern-
ing public auctions of cocoa. One bylaw provides that, unless other-
wise arranged, cocoa shall be delivered from the seller's stores on
surrender of a delivery order, and that the seller shall pay for its
transfer into the buyer's truck. The decision is designed to clarify
uncertainty in the matter.

NIGERIA EXPORTS MORE CACAO IN 1957;
NOW COMBATING DISEASE AND INSECTS

Nigerian exports of cocoa beans in 1957 amounted to 303,078,000 pounds, compared with 261,930,000 pounds in 1956. Exports to the United Kingdom were the largest--accounting for 133,063,000 pounds. The United States was the next largest market, taking 57 million pounds. The value of Nigeria's 1957 cocoa bean exports increased 8.5 percent over 1956.

The Western Region Ministry of Agriculture and Natural Resources has approved a plan for an intensive survey of swollen-shoot-infected cacao areas, and is considering demonstrations in the areas with a view to getting infected farms back into economic production.

Nigerian farmers did not buy chemicals and sprayers to control capsids in 1957 to any extent, even though the Western Region arranged to lend them the money. Cacao trees now are showing damage from capsid attacks last July and August. However, arrangements again are being made to offer loans to farmers for chemicals and sprayers, and the spray program is expected to be operating by this July.

CUBA AUTHORIZES TRANSFER OF
CERTAIN SUGAR QUOTAS

The Cuban Sugar Stabilization Institute has authorized sugar mills in Oriente Province to transfer to other mills their share of the 1958 production quotas they are unable to meet.

In late March, saboteurs destroyed about 19,000 short tons of bagged sugar at Central Elia. This quantity is equivalent to about half the sugar manufactured thus far this season by this mill, or about one-third of its output in 1957. Rebel activity to date, however, has not interfered materially with Cuba's production of its set limit of 6,250,000 tons of sugar this season.

The Sugar Stabilization Institute also has decided that any sugar set aside for local consumption in 1958 and not sold by December 31, 1958, automatically will be transferred to the U. S. Free Sugar Quota. The local consumption quota for 1958 has been set at 336,000 short tons. Authorized sales for local consumption probably will be less.

Each year, some domestic needs are met by sugar manufactured outside of legal quotas. Such illegal production is known locally as "bibijagua" sugar. This year, with total legal production limited by quota and with surplus cane available, there will be greater temptation to convert some of this cane into unregistered sugar. Any sugar so produced and used will reduce the need for legally allocated sugar for local consumption. Local consumption of legally allocated sugar in 1957 was about 330,000 short tons.

PHILIPPINE FOOD AND EXPORT CROPS
AFFECTED BY DROUGHT

Lack of rain has seriously affected the Philippine Republic's production of its principal food crops and some important export crops. Rainfall
in 1957 was 40 percent below normal, and drought conditions which lasted
throughout the year have continued well into 1958.

According to official estimates, the 1957-58 rice crop will be 4 percent below the 1956-57 harvest, while the corn crop will decline by 3 percent. However, in view of the extensive drought damage, these two crops
may be even smaller. If so, the import requirement of 174,000 tons of rice,
as estimated by the National Rice and Corn Corporation, will probably not
meet the country's needs.

Production of coconuts for copra, coconut oil, and desiccated coconut--
the country's largest single source of export earnings--is expected to be
off 25 to 30 percent for the first half of 1958. Output in the second half
of the year will also be down unless there is adequate rainfall soon.

Tobacco production is expected to be down, but the sugarcane crop
does not appear to have been seriously damaged thus far. However, continued dry weather would reduce the crop substantially.

CANE AND SUGAR PRODUCTION IN
CUBA AND PHILIPPINES

As Cuba and the Philippines are the two major sources of U. S. sugar
imports, the following table (page 18) showing production and output may
be of interest.

Cuba has about 3.5 million acres of sugarcane. However, Cuba is
limiting 1958 production of sugar to 6,250,000 short tons, raw value.
Estimates indicate that with normal yields, this restricted output could
be obtained by harvesting 3.1 million acres and processing 49 million
short tons of sugarcane.

Philippine sugar production for the 1957-58 crop is expected to be
1,313,000 short tons, raw value, an increase of 170,000 tons over 1956-57
production. The 1956-57 output was smaller mainly as a result of reduced
planted acreage; the drought during 1957 also may have had an effect.
This year, planted acreage is up, and an increase in cane cut and sugar
produced is expected.

SUGARCANE: Cuba, acreage, production, and sugar output, 1950-58

Crop year [1]	Acreage in cane		Sugarcane harvested		Raw sugar produced	
	Grown	Harvested	Per acre	Total [2]	Total	Per ton of sugarcane [2]
	1,000 acres	1,000 acres	Short tons	1,000 s. tons	1,000 s. tons	Pounds
1950	3,014	2,948	15.91	46,916	6,126	261
1951	3,117	3,096	16.00	49,537	6,349	256
1952	3,521	3,474	18.89	65,629	7,964	243
1953	3,921	2,156	20.88	45,010	5,687	253
1954	3,331	2,310	18.75	43,317	5,398	249
1955	3,066	2,059	18.64	38,381	5,001	261
1956	3,252	2,252	18.12	40,798	5,229	256
1957	3,196	2,998	16.44	49,289	6,252	254
1958 [3]	3,499	[4]	[4]	[4]	[5] 6,250	[4]

[1] Harvesting usually begins in January and extends through June. The length of the growing season is normally 12 months.
[2] Cane production for some of the early years includes cane for invert molasses.
[3] Preliminary. [4] Not available.
[5] Restricted maximum authorized.

SUGARCANE: Philippines, acreage, production, and sugar output, 1950-57

Crop year [1]	Sugarcane				Sugar produced		
	Acreage		Production				
	Total	Harvested for centrifugal sugar	Yield per acre [2]	Total	Centrifugal as made	Muscovada and Panocha	Centrifugal sugar made per ton sugarcane
	1,000 acres	1,000 acres	Short tons	1,000 short tons	1,000 short tons	1,000 short tons	Pounds
1950	417	382	21.41	8,177	935	51	229
1951	496	466	21.36	9,952	1,077	62	216
1952	547	517	20.21	10,447	1,134	63	217
1953	575	545	23.92	13,038	1,434	60	220
1954	570	540	23.18	12,516	1,372	55	219
1955	500	469	23.18	10,871	1,219	60	224
1956	475	443	23.41	10,369	1,143	70	220
1957 [3]	480	452	23.90	10,805	1,313	70	243

[1] Harvesting begins in October. The length of the growing season is about 11 months.
[2] Cane production divided by harvested acreage.
[3] Preliminary.

INDIA FAVORS SUBSIDIZED
SUGAR EXPORTS

The Indian Government is considering legislation to encourage exports of sugar at subsidized prices, according to A. P. Jain, Minister of Food and Agriculture. At a meeting of the Indian Sugar Mills Association, Mr. Jain defended the recent increase in excise duty as necessary to restrict domestic consumption in order to permit exports of sugar.

B. S. Sawhney, presiding at the meeting, said India earned over Rs. 120 million (about $25.2 million) of foreign exchange from 1957 sugar exports, and needs a permanent sugar export market. India's centrifugal sugar production has doubled since 1953.

The meeting called upon the government by resolution to check production of Khandsari by licensing, and to levy an excise duty on units using power to prevent its competition with factory sugar. Khandsari is a white sugar produced by cottage industry.

GREECE EXPECTS TO INCREASE
RICE ACREAGE

Rice acreage in Greece now being planted is expected to be slightly larger than a year ago. Several reasons for the increase are given: (1) prices to growers are satisfactory; (2) production costs are decreasing as more land is irrigated; (3) domestic production does not meet requirements; (4) prices of imported rice are higher than for domestic rice; and (5) demand for rice seed is good.

The seed production service of the Ministry of Agriculture has provided growers with about 1,790,000 pounds of improved seed, compared with 1,100,000 pounds in 1957. With the exception of 6,600 pounds of "Bersani," the seed is "Americano," which is well adapted to local soil and climate. The seed provided is very popular with growers.

The 1957 crop was around 130 million pounds of rough rice, 25 percent more than in 1956. Thus, the downward trend in rice acreage since 1954 was halted. Expansion prior to 1954 was partly speculative, and when prices declined growers reduced acreage.

Rice imports into Greece in 1957 of 10,886 metric tons were from the following countries (metric tons): Egypt, 5,634; Thailand, 1,760; United States, 1,622; Netherlands, 654; Italy, 232, and other countries, 984. Rice exports in 1957 were only 960 metric tons.

In 1958, 5,000 tons of U. S. rice are to be imported through the International Cooperation Administration, probably after July 1. Carryover stocks at the end of 1958 are expected to exceed those at the end of 1957.

VENEZUELA TO IMPORT RICE
UNTIL OWN CROP REGAINED

Venezuela expects to import at least 20,000 metric tons of rice in 1958 and possibly more in 1959. Rice crop losses in 1957 as a result of the "hoja blanca" disease have caused not only a shortage of rice this year but also a reduction in acreage about to be planted.

Meanwhile, several new varieties resistant to the disease are reported to have been developed at the Palo Gordo rice farm, Rockefeller International Basic Economy Corporation. The following varieties are cited: Colusa, Asahi, La crosse, La crosse x Magnolia, Missouri R-500, Bruin sel. x Zenith, Hgb. Mix. 11-49-19-5, and B53-2604 B438A Rogue.

Most of these are medium or short-grain varieties. Venezuelan consumers in recent years have preferred long-grain varieties. However, the Palo Gordo farm now has sufficient seed of the preferred La Crosse and La Crosse x 253 varieties to plant 1,000 hectares (2,470 acres). Enough seed is expected to be harvested from the area to plant from 15,000 to 20,000 hectares (35,000 to 50,000 acres) in 1959.

After the development of the "hoja blanca" disease-resistant varieties was announced, the Venezuelan Development Corporation reconsidered the recent suspension of its rice program (see Foreign Crops and Markets, April 7, 1958). An important reason for the abandonment of the program was the damage caused by "hoja blanca."

U. S. RICE EXPORTS
UP IN FEBRUARY

Rice exports from the United States in February were 1,109,000 (100 pounds) in terms of milled rice, the largest since last November. Over half of exports were to Pakistan, and a third to Cuba.

Current statistics have recently become available from the Census Bureau for shipments of Section 416 donations. These data and the revised monthly total exports of rice for August through February are shown below:

Item	Aug.	Sept.	Oct.	Nov.	Dec.	Jan.	Feb.
	1,000 bags	1,000 bags	1,000 bags	1,000 bags	1,000 bags	1,000 bags	1,000 bags
Exports.........	379	1,472	947	980	864	539	1,108
Donations.......	47	52	185	164	88	36	1
Total......	426	1,524	1,132	1,144	952	575	1,109

Source: Bureau of the Census.

RICE: United States exports in terms of milled, to specified countries, February 1958, with comparisons 1/

Country of destination	August–July		August–February			February 2/	
	1955-56	1956-57	1955-56	1956-57	1957-58 2/	1957	1958
	1,000 bags	1,000 bags	1,000 bags	1,000 bags	1,000 bags	1,000 bags	1,000 bags
Western Hemisphere:							
Canada	397	376	301	221	213	31	14
British Honduras	35	33	25	8	6	0	6
British West Indies	8	137	6	84	97	2	2
El Salvador	44	1	2	0	0	0	0
Cuba	2,927	4,054	2,004	2,621	2,688	478	377
Haiti	5	58	2	55	3	44	2
Netherlands Antilles	28	42	18	23	31	4	8
Bolivia	191	176	153	176	22	0	0
Colombia	13	3	10	1	3/	0	0
Surinam	0	20	0	20	3/	0	0
Venezuela	32	40	16	19	2	15	0
Other countries	148	79	27	50	50	3	3
Total	3,828	5,019	2,564	3,278	3,112	577	412
Europe:							
Belgium–Luxembourg	285	686	152	496	52	61	8
France	78	1	3/	1	0	0	0
West Germany	53	20	27	2	0	3/	0
Netherlands	31	50	5	50	3	0	0
Sweden	9	16	8	13	8	1	3/
Switzerland	22	58	17	56	30	4	0
Other countries	10	39	3	26	12	4	5
Total	488	870	212	644	105	70	13
Asia:							
India	215	4,376	215	2,301	0	856	0
Indochina	220	10	220	10	3/	0	0
Indonesia	516	5,424	0	4,872	0	33	0
Japan	2,383	109	2,381	92	3	1	3/
Korean Republic	1	2,746	0	90	242	85	0
Pakistan	2,653	4,372	0	3,221	2,005	137	644
Philippine Republic	28	20	22	20	377	0	3/
Ryukyu Islands	0 4/	207	0 4/	201	0	0	0
Saudi Arabia	75	98	63	78	86	25	3/
Other Arabian States	0	22	0	17	107	2	2
Other countries	38	226	13	226	4	1	1
Total	6,129	17,610	2,914	11,124	2,824	1,140	647
Total Oceania................	39	47	21	28	31	5	3
French West Africa	625	0	416	0	0	0	0
Liberia	276	248	118	92	197	4	30
Other Africa	21	19	14	10	8	1	1
Destination not specified	26	13	12	7	12	0	2
Total	11,432	23,826	6,271	15,183	6,289	1,797	1,108
Section 416 donations	967	2,036	0	1,850	572	152	1
Ground rough rice for animal feed:	514	288	0	–	0	0	0
World total	12,913	26,150	6,271	17,033	6,861	1,949	1,109

1/ Includes brown, broken, screenings and brewers' rice and rough rice converted to terms of milled at 65 percent. 2/ Preliminary. 3/ Less than 500 cwt. 4/ Shipped by Army under contract with International Cooperation Administration.

Source: Bureau of the Census and Department of Agriculture.

PHILIPPINE RICE CROP
REDUCED BY DROUGHT

The Philippine rice crop of 1957-58 was reduced about 4 percent by drought, according to an official estimate of late March. Production was given as 7,100 million pounds of rough rice (2,200,000 metric tons) compared with the record crop in 1956-57 of 7,416.6 million pounds (2,290,000 tons).

It now appears the crop was less than the latest official estimate. Drought damage has been extensive. The National Rice and Corn Corporation is now estimating about 174,000 tons of milled rice will have to be imported in 1958.

JAPAN REPORTS WHEAT AND BARLEY
PURCHASES FOR 1957-58

The Japanese Ministry of Agriculture and Forestry reports that Japan's foreign purchases of wheat and barley in the fiscal year ended March 31 totaled 81.3 million bushels and 35.1 million bushels, respectively.

Japan bought 39.6 million bushels of U. S. wheat--over half of its total wheat imports. This quantity was made up of 29.7 million bushels of Western White, 8.0 million bushels of Hard Winter, and 1.9 million bushels of Dark Northern Spring. Japanese wheat purchases from Canada totaled 35.9 million bushels, and from Australia 5.8 million.

Japan's largest supplier of barley was the United States, with 15.6 million bushels (11.1 million bushels of two-rowed, 4.5 million bushels of Western). Canada supplied 10.2 million bushels, Australia 9.2 million bushels, and Iraq 92,000 bushels.

BRITISH TESTING NEW
SUGAR BEET SEED

Experimental quantities of a promising new sugar beet seed have been delivered to factories in the United Kingdom, according to British plant breeders. The new seed is said to yield considerably more than ordinary seed, with a uniform crop of early, vigorous growth. It can be used in precision drills.

The seed's qualities are attributed to its being a triploid; that is, each seed has 3 times the basic number of hereditary factors, or 3 sets or chromosomes. Ordinary seed has only twice the basic number.

A published report by the British plant breeders says that it is too early to estimate the increased yield on a field scale. However, trials so far indicate it is 12 percent above ordinary seed. Trials in 7 European countries yielded 8 percent more than polyploid varieties.

WESTERN EUROPE'S WHEAT
PROSPECTS MOSTLY GOOD

In Western Europe, conditions during the fall and winter were
mostly favorable for winter grain crops, and little winterkill has
been reported. Unseasonably low temperatures during late March and
early April in some countries, however, caused concern that crops
may have suffered some damage during that period. The late cold spell
slowed growth of winter grains and delayed spring work in a number
of countries. No appraisal of the overall effects of the cold is
yet available.

It appears that wheat acreage may be close to the large acreage
last year in the most important producing countries. Production
prospects were good up to the time of the cold spell. If it develops
that damage was slight and if conditions are favorable for the
remainder of the growing season, Western Europe's total wheat crop
could be large, as it was last year.

In the principal producing countries, latest information is:

In France, a slight increase in winter wheat acreage and favorable fall and winter conditions led to expectations of a 1958 wheat
crop larger than the record 1957 harvest. However, since the cold
spell of late March, comments, though optimistic, are more guarded.
Crop development is now said to be about 3 weeks late, and unless
made up by the end of June, the crop will be susceptible to scorching.

In February, before the cold checked growth of winter wheat and
slowed field work, Italy expected a record harvest in 1958. No appraisal of the cold weather's effect on the final outturn is yet
available.

Wheat acreage in Spain is expected to be about the same as in
1957. A shortage of rain, especially in areas north of Madrid, is
handicapping development. Germination and growth in northern districts were estimated in early February at only 90 percent of normal.
Development of the crop south of Madrid has been good.

Development of winter grain is backward in West Germany, but
winter losses have been small and the overall outlook appears good.
Winter wheat in the United Kingdom was in generally satisfactory
condition at the beginning of April, according to official accounts.
As in other areas, an unseasonably cold spring has handicapped opti-
mum development.

Wheat acreage in Greece is about 3 percent less than the large
1957 acreage. Adverse weather at seeding time caused the reduction.
Wider distribution of seed of selected varieties and a continuing
increase in the use of fertilizer improve yield prospects. (Continued)

These six countries together normally account for almost 90 percent of Western Europe's total wheat production. Scattered reports on conditions in Eastern Europe indicate that spring work there, too, is behind schedule because of unfavorable weather. Yugoslavia, one of the leading producers of the area, reports a 7-percent increase over the 1957 acreage of winter wheat. Reports in February stated that wheat plants were small at that time, with less than normal stooling.

CUBA EXPECTED TO IMPORT MORE
DUTY-FREE CORN FROM U. S.

Cuba still faces a shortage of corn (see Foreign Crops and Markets, December 2, 1957), due partially to rapid growth of its broiler industry, and will probably need to import about a million bushels between now and August.

Decrees issued on January 10 and February 18 each authorized duty-free imports of 200,000 Spanish quintals (362,000 bushels) of U. S. shelled corn. Practically all imports thus authorized have been received, but corn supplies are still tight. It therefore seems likely that Cuba will continue to authorize duty-free imports of corn, as they are required, until the next harvest. (The import duty is $.69 per bushel.) On shipments made under the January and February decrees, authorized importers are reported to have paid $2.10 to $2.21 per bushel for U. S. corn delivered at truck.

U. S. JULY-MARCH WHEAT AND FLOUR
EXPORTS DOWN 28 PERCENT

United States wheat and flour exports during July-March of 1957-58 are estimated at 286 million bushels, compared with 398 million bushels during the same period a year earlier. This represents a reduction of about 28 percent, due mostly to reduced demands for wheat in Western Europe, which had a record crop in 1957.

This preliminary figure of exports during July-March, including inspections of grain and estimates of flour exported in March, shows substantial reductions to France, West Germany, Belgium-Luxembourg, Yugoslavia, the United Kingdom, and the Netherlands.

Exports to some countries, however, are above those a year ago. India's purchases of U. S. wheat were almost double those of last year. Exports to Brazil, Morocco, and Colombia also increased. Poland took 18 million bushels during July-March 1957-58. This is the first time in over 5 years that Poland has taken any U. S. wheat.

Official export data for 1957-58 are available only through February.

WHEAT AND FLOUR: United States exports by countries of destination,
July-February 1956-57 and July-February 1957-58

Destination	July-February 1956-57			July-February 1957-58		
	Wheat	Flour 1/	Total	Wheat	Flour 1/	Total
			1,000 bushels, grain equivalent			
Western Hemisphere:						
Central America ....:	893	2,675	3,568	896	3,158	4,054
Cuba ....:	2,062	2,622	4,684	2,051	3,091	5,142
British West Indies ....:	2	2,364	2,366	2	2,295	2,297
Haiti ....:	--	864	864	156	1,086	1,242
Colombia ....:	2,317	40	2,357	3,243	433	3,676
Venezuela ....:	151	4,258	4,409	522	4,269	4,791
Peru ....:	2,139	181	2,320	2,771	218	2,989
Bolivia ....:	2,454	838	3,292	--	314	314
Chile ....:	4,883	19	4,902	1,968	74	2,042
Brazil ....:	4,556	1	4,557	8,571	1,388	9,959
Others ....:	1,154	1,880	3,034	482	1,639	2,121
Total ....:	20,611	15,742	36,353	20,662	17,965	38,627
Europe:						
Norway ....:	1,389	570	1,959	45	604	649
Denmark ....:	3,137	26	3,163	1,240	9	1,249
United Kingdom ....:	27,262	880	28,142	14,421	642	15,063
Netherlands ....:	15,475	2,324	17,799	2,461	2,504	4,965
Belgium-Luxembourg .....:	16,330	19	16,349	1,573	16	1,589
France ....:	29,303	1	29,304	--	6	6
Germany, West ....:	28,379	83	28,462	14,037	35	14,072
Austria ....:	1,853	3	1,856	1,117	--	1,117
Switzerland ....:	6,472	6	6,478	437	--	437
Finland ....:	2,813	--	2,813	681	--	681
Poland ....:	--	--	-	18,479	--	18,479
Portugal ....:	4,635	79	4,714	287	64	351
Italy ....:	5,655	252	5,907	742	473	1,215
Yugoslavia ....:	11,313	12	11,325	3,031	26	3,057
Greece ....:	11,217	21	11,238	1,513	3	1,516
Others ....:	1,964	50	2,014	2,097	370	2,467
Total ....:	167,197	4,326	171,523	62,161	4,752	66,913
Asia:						
Turkey ....:	9,200	--	9,200	1,957	--	1,957
Lebanon ....:	--	1,504	1,504	--	1,195	1,195
Israel ....:	7,359	479	7,838	5,888	7	5,895
Saudi Arabia ....:	959	2,607	3,566	14	983	997
India ....:	27,037	22	27,059	61,087	19	61,106
Pakistan ....:	17,767	1	17,768	11,912	1	11,913
Vietnam, Laos, and						
Cambodia ....:	--	2,336	2,336	--	665	665
Indonesia ....:	--	3,733	3,733	--	99	99
Philippine Republic ....:	--	4,336	4,336	--	5,501	5,501
Korea ....:	7,213	654	7,867	5,006	803	5,809
Formosa ....:	4,156	--	4,156	4,677	4	4,681
Japan ....:	31,299	1,360	32,659	29,144	1,442	30,586
Others ....:	861	782	1,643	1,880	1,545	3,425
Total ....:	105,851	17,814	123,665	121,565	12,264	133,829
Africa:						
Morocco ....:	--	21	21	1,448	8	1,456
Tunisia ....:	2,580	2	2,582	102	110	212
Egypt ....:	1,071	358	1,429	--	326	326
French West Africa .....:	1,924	6	1,930	458	1	459
Ghana ....:	--	951	951	--	1,097	1,097
Western British Africa..:	--	1,262	1,262	--	1,454	1,454
Others ....:	1,349	1,209	2,558	298	966	1,264
Total ....:	6,924	3,809	10,733	2,306	3,962	6,268
Oceania ....:	--	32	32	--	21	21
Unspecified 2/ ....:	1,115	2,783	3,898	395	10,162	10,557
World total ....:	301,698	44,506	346,204	207,089	49,126	256,215

1/ Wholly of U.S. wheat. Beginning July 1, 1957, the factor for converting
100 pounds of flour into bushels of grain equivalent changed from 2.33 to 2.3.
2/ Includes shipments for relief or charity which are not shown by destination.

BRAZIL PLANS IMPORTS OF 1,611,000 TONS
OF WHEAT IN 1958

Brazil's planned wheat imports for 1958 total 1,611,000 metric tons (59.2 million bushels) from all countries. Commercial availability from the country's 1957 crop, most of it harvested last December, is estimated at 600,000 metric tons (22.0 million bushels). Adding planned imports, the total supply for the year would be 2,211,000 tons (81.2 million bushels).

WHEAT: Brazil's planned imports, 1958

Months	Argentina 1/	Uruguay	U. S. P. L. 480	Others 2/	Total
	Metric tons	Metric tons	Metric tons	Metric tons	Metric tons
March............:	46,000	---	---	---	66,000
April............:	150,000	---	---	20,000	170,000
May..............:	75,000	---	100,000	30,000	205,000
June.............:	50,000	15,000	100,000	---	165,000
July.............:	50,000	15,000	125,000	---	190,000
August...........:	50,000	15,000	125,000	---	190,000
September........:	50,000	15,000	125,000	---	190,000
October..........:	50,000	15,000	125,000	20,000	210,000
November 3/ .....:	100,000	15,000	4/ 80,000	30,000	225,000
Total........:	641,000	90,000	780,000	100,000	1,611,000

Source: Wheat Expansion Service and Brazilian Foreign Office.

1/ 66,000 tons from the March quota and 125,000 tons from the April quota were shipped under the 1957 bilateral agreement. The balance of the shipments (April through November) will be credited to the 1958 agreement quota.

2/ The scheduled April-May international market quota is in fulfillment of the 1957 normal market obligation and the October-November quota in fulfillment of the 1958 obligation.

3/ No imports scheduled after November 1958 because of desire to complete imports before harvesting of the domestic wheat crop.

4/ The 80,000 tons of U. S. wheat scheduled for November is the 1958 U. S. dollar normal market portion of the P. L. 480 Agreement.

INDIA'S WHEAT PRODUCTION REDUCED

The first official estimate places India's 1958 wheat acreage at 29,576,000 acres compared with the corresponding 1957 estimate of 30,782,000 acres. India's first estimate of grain acreage does not cover the entire country's acreage but is usually about 90 percent of the total finally reported.

The decrease in Indian acreage for the current year is attributed to lack of monsoon rains at seeding time in some parts of the country. The principal districts reporting reduced acreage are Bihar, Madhya Pradesh, Uttar Pradesh, and Rajasthan. Some increase in the wheat acreage of the Punjab and Himachal Pradesh partly offset the reduction in dry areas.

Condition of the crop is described as generally satisfactory except in the dry districts mentioned above. The drought there has been prolonged, and as a result, private forecasts of the harvest now underway are significantly below the country's 1957 final estimate of 338 million bushels.

U. S. EXPORTS OF AMERICAN-
EGYPTIAN DOWN IN FEBRUARY

Exports of American-Egyptian cotton were 1,483 bales (500 pounds gross) in February 1958, compared with 2,878 bales in January, and 4,330 bales in February 1957. The United Kingdom received 1,416 bales of the February exports, and the remaining 67 bales went to France.

Exports during August-February 1957-58 were 9,099 bales, compared with 45,445 bales in the corresponding period of 1956-57. The United Kingdom and France received the largest quantities of the August-February exports, with smaller quantities going to Austria, Chile, West Germany, and Italy.

CANADA'S COTTON CONSUMPTION
AT SAME LEVEL IN MARCH

Canada's cotton consumption, based on bale openings, was 26,000 bales (500 pounds gross) during March 1958, the same level as in February, although 16 percent below the 31,000 bales consumed in March 1957. Consumption during August-March 1957-58 was 231,000 bales, against 261,000 bales in the corresponding period of 1956-57.

INDIA ALLOWS FURTHER IMPORTS
OF STERLING-AREA COTTON

The Government of India announced on April 6, 1958, that licenses would be granted for imports of an additional 30,000 bales (400 pounds gross) of sterling-area cotton stapling 1-3/16 inches and above. Import licenses will be issued to mills only, on the basis of their consumption of Sudanese and Egyptian cotton during the last 3 seasons, 1954-55 through 1956-57, and will be valid for shipment up to July 31, 1958.

Cotton qualifying under this allocation include Egyptian, Sudanese, Peruvian, and East African.

U. S. COTTON LINTERS EXPORTS
CONTINUE TO DECLINE

United States exports of cotton linters, mostly chemical qualities, were 16,000 bales (500 pounds gross) in February 1958, down 27 percent from January exports of 22,000 bales, and 65 percent below the 46,000 bales exported in February 1957. Exports during August-February 1957-58 were 155,000 bales, compared with 269,000 bales during the corresponding period a year earlier.

Principal destinations of linters exports in August-February 1957-58, with comparable 1956-57 figures in parentheses, were: West Germany 59,000 bales (90,000); Netherlands 30,000 (44,000); United Kingdom 28,000 (44,000); and Canada 17,000 (23,000).

EGYPT'S 1957-58 COTTON
CROP ABOVE PREVIOUS YEAR'S

Egypt's 1957-58 cotton production, according to the fourth and final official estimate issued April 15, 1958, is 1,861,000 bales (500 pounds gross). This is 25 percent larger than the 1956-57 crop of 1,492,000 bales.

Most of the increase this season was in the extra-long staple varieties, Karnak and Menoufi, and the long staples such as Ashmouni. Production of medium-long staple Giza cotton declined 13 percent

COTTON: Egypt, production by staple length and variety,
final official estimates, 1956-57 and 1957-58

Staple length and principal varieties	1956-57	1957-58	Percent change
	1,000 bales 1/	1,000 bales 1/	
Extra long staple, over 1-3/8":			
Karnak and Menoufi...............:	611	844	+38
Medium long staple, over 1-1/4":			
Giza 30, 31, and 47.............:	272	236	-13
Long staple, over 1-1/8":			
Ashmouni.......................:	574	741	+29
Total.....................:	1,457	1,821	+25
Scarto (unclassified cotton)........:	35	40	+14
Total.....................:	1,492	1,861	+25

1/ Bales of 500 pounds gross.
Source: Government of Egypt.

RANCE TO HAVE SHARP INCREASE
N 1958 OILSEED PRODUCTION

Production in France of edible oilseeds--predominantly rapeseed--is forecast
or the current year at around 275,000 short tons, a sharp increase from the
01,000 tons produced in 1957.

Approximately 370,000 acres were seeded to winter rapeseed for harvest this
pring. This estimated acreage is more than half again the acreage harvested in
957; freeze damage reduced the area only slightly. Rapeseed production forecasts
or 1958 range from 240,000 to 260,000 tons.

Flaxseed production in 1958 is forecast at 1.6 million bushels, up about 5
ercent from 1957 and over 10 percent above the 1.4 million bushels produced in
956. About one-third of the French flaxseed outturn is from flax grown for
iber and two-thirds is from flax grown for seed.

Production of edible oilseeds in 1957 was up sharply from the low production
evel of 1956, when freezing weather severely damaged the rapeseed crop and thus
aterially reduced the total outturn of edible oilseeds.

OILSEEDS: France, acreage, yield, and production, 1956 and 1957

Oilseed	Area harvested		Yield per acre		Production	
	1956 1/	1957 2/	1956 1/	1957 2/	1956 1/	1957 2/
	Acres	Acres	Pounds	Pounds	Short tons	Short tons
Edible:						
Rapeseed:						
Colza..........	123,500	231,200	130.3	136.6	80,750	157,840
Navette........	19,270	17,040	86.6	77.3	8,320	6,330
Total........	142,770	248,240	---	---	89,070	164,170
Poppyseed..........	1,980	990	68.7	73.2	680	375
Sunflower seed.....	13,830	5,930	133.0	125.0	8,850	3,650
Others 3/..........	36,300	75,800	84.0	87.0	15,350	33,000
Total edible.	194,880	330,960	---	---	113,950	201,195
			Bushels	Bushels	Bushels	Bushels
Industrial:						
Flaxseed.........	4/ 143,000	4/130,000	9.6	11.3	1,375,000	1,467,000

1/ Revised. 2/ Preliminary. 3/ Includes mustard seed, which probably accounts for
ost of this category. 4/ Acreage for seed and fiber.

ompiled from official and other sources.

COLOMBIA REORGANIZES ITS AGRICULTURAL
TRADING ORGANIZATION

On April 11, the Colombian Government reorganized its Ministry of
Agriculture's trading organization and changed its name from the Coro-
racion de Defensa de Productos Agricolas to the Corporacion de
Abastecimientos (INA), which it had been called some time previously.

The organization's main functions are to facilitate production, distribution, importation, and exportation of agricultural commodities.
INA regulates prices, while avoiding speculation, by buying and selling
foreign and domestic agricultural products.

The organization is divided into two permanent committees. One
will be in charge of buying, selling, and prices, and the other in
charge of investment, capital and reserves, and storage facilities.

Half of the profits of INA would go to the Agricultural Credit
Bank, and the remainder used for loans, depreciation reserves, pay-
ments to stockholders, recapitalization, and aid to production. The
organization's authorized capital is 50 million pesos (about U.S. $7
million).

PHILIPPINE COPRA EXPORTS
LOWER IN MARCH

Philippine copra exports in March declined for the fourth suc-
cessive month to 54,658 long tons, the smallest monthly tonnage since
May 1955. Coconut oil exports of 3,624 tons were the smallest monthly
volume reported since January 1954. Combined March exports of copra
and coconut oil totaled 38,059 tons, oil basis, a decrease of one-
eighth from February shipments.

Cumulative January-March exports of copra were 183,031 tons, less
than four-fifths the quantity shipped in the first quarter of 1957.

January-March coconut oil exports of 16,466 tons were just two-
thirds of the total shipments in the comparable period of 1957. The
decline in copra and coconut oil shipments may be attributed to
drought.

The Philippine copra export price in mid-April was about $183 per
short ton c.i.f. Pacific Coast (mid-March - $177, mid-February $179).
Local buying prices were reported at 30 to 36 pesos per 100 kilograms
($152.41 to $182.89 per long ton) resecada Manila and producing areas.

COPRA: Philippine Republic, exports by country of destination,
March and January-March for years 1957 and 1958

Country	1957 1/		1958 1/	
	March	January-March	March	January-March
	Long tons	Long tons	Long tons	Long tons
North America:				
United States......... ....:	17,608	71,940	20,804	49,413
Atlantic Coast...................:	(2,750)	(7,284)	(---)	(---)
Pacific Coast...................:	(14,858)	(64,656)	(20,804)	(49,413)
Canada...........................:	500	4,450	---	1,800
Total.......................:	18,108	76,390	20,804	51,213
South America:				
Colombia........................ :	1,000	10,000	6,184	15,753
Venezuela.... .... :	1,500	8,700	---	1,500
Total.......................:	2,500	18,700	6,184	17,253
Europe:				
Belgium..........................:	1,000	2,000	---	---
Denmark..........................:	1,000	7,375	1,000	4,800
France...........................:	---	---	750	3,310
Germany, West....................:	4,634	15,634	1,500	15,965
Italy............................:	---	10,687	---	1,400
Netherlands......................:	35,351	88,299	11,100	55,793
Norway...........................:	4,401	8,001	---	500
Sweden...........................:	5,000	8,300	---	500
Optional discharge 2/.............:	---	---	9,800	26,577
Total.......................:	51,386	140,296	24,150	108,845
Asia:				
Israel...........................:	---	---	3,020	3,020
Lebanon..........................:	---	---	500	2,700
Total.......................:	---	---	3,520	5,720
Grand total.....................:	71,994	235,386	54,658	183,031

1/ Preliminary. 2/ West Germany, Netherlands or Belgium.
Source: Philippine trade sources.

COCONUT OIL: Philippine Republic, exports by country of destination,
March and January-March for years 1957 and 1958

Country	1957 1/		1958 1/	
	March	January-March	March	January-March
	Long tons	Long tons	Long tons	Long tons
North America:				
United States.....................:	4,582	16,985	3,274	16,116
Atlantic Coast...................:	(4,582)	(16,634)	(3,274)	(16,116)
Pacific Coast...................:	(---)	(351)	(---)	(---)
Cuba.............................:	---	345	350	350
Total........................:	4,582	17,330	3,624	16,466
Europe:				
Germany, West....................:	---	1,427	---	---
Netherlands......................:	3,299	5,945	---	---
Total........................:	3,299	7,372	---	---
Grand total.....................:	7,881	24,702	3,624	16,466

1/ Preliminary.

Source: Philippine trade sources.

CPSIA information can be obtained
at www.ICGtesting.com
Printed in the USA
BVHW031222021118
531991BV00008B/736/P